GRANADA

First published in Great Britain in 2003
By Granada Media, an imprint of Andre Deutsch Limited
20 Mortimer Street
London W1T 3JW

Text copyright LWT © 2003. Ant and Dec's Saturday Night
Takeaway is an LWT production for itv1.

Photographs © Granada Media 2003

With thanks to CBBC and Ben Productions LLC for the
kind permission to feature Bill and Ben.

Text written by Trevor Baker

A catalogue record is available from the British Library.

ISBN 0 23300 057 7

Printed and bound in the UK.

Project Editors: Gillian Holmes, Lorna Russell
Art Editor: Vicky Holmes
Designer: Simon Mercer
Production: Lisa Moore

Contents

We were going to
use something bigger
but we couldn't
be bothered

Introduction

When we first came up with the idea for *Saturday Night Takeaway* we thought to ourselves: 'OK, it's a variety show that winks very heavily back to the kind of shows we loved when we were growing up. Do people want this? We don't know!'

We remember watching *Game For A Laugh* and when they walked down the stairs at the beginning it looked like they were having such a good time.

So, now that *Saturday Night Takeaway* is about to reach its third series it's probably OK for us to admit that we only did it 'cos we liked the idea of getting paid to dress up like fools, meet some of the world's biggest stars, and make ourselves look completely ridiculous for your entertainment. Of course at times it's a lot harder work than we ever thought it was going to be. When we've been in the make-up chair for four hours being transformed into middle-aged Jamaican women, or when Little Ant and Dec have been flicking bogeys at us for half an hour, we do wonder what we're doing.

I mean, we even give ourselves over to the mercy of long-suffering producers of the show for 'What's Next' and there is some trepidation when you take the earpiece out and you don't know what's going to happen, but that's what live telly's all about, being spontaneous, thinking on your feet and having a laugh. It's good, because we do hits on people with the 'Undercover' segment of the show, but we prove that we can take it, too.

The sketches revisited in this book are some of our favourites and in here you'll find us flying around the world for a five minute gag at Simon Cowell's expense, transforming ourselves into increasingly bizarre characters, and giving away the contents of an entire prime time advert break.

Amongst other things we've ended up grooming some very dubious gorillas, dancing with the Moulin Rouge, dressing up as Bill and Ben the Flowerpot Men and having a circus freak attack us with a lobster. It's all here, with pictures to prove that, yes, it actually happened and with a running commentary from us, explaining exactly what it feels like to have 'the lobsters of doom' doing the fandango up and down your spine. And if we do end up looking silly, remember we're doing it for you!

We've always wanted to do a Saturday night prime time show, it's a bit of a dream come true. It's our favourite show. It's the one that we enjoy the most, that we put the most into, and that we get the most out of and for people to be enjoying it as well... it's just brilliant.

Ant and Dec
2003

Undercover
Pop Idol: Germany

At the beginning of 2003 Pop Idol fever was sweeping the world. Even in Germany, apparently, new stars were being made, as daytime TV titans Philip Schofield and Fern Britton were about to discover on 'This Morning'.

'When ITVs reality music show *Pop Idol* started a mere 16 months ago we knew that it was going to be big,' says Philip sitting on the sofa with Fern and DJ Neil 'Dr' Fox, 'but we did not know what it was going to spawn.'

The camera cuts to a dressing room where the world's ugliest pop stars, two Germans called Gustav and Jurgen, are sitting eating frankfurters out of a jar.

'After conquering the States,' explains Philip, 'it travelled over the water to our German cousins, where it got a little bit more ... **unusual**.'

Just how unusual is illustrated by a shot of Gustav and Jurgen holding hands at the final of *Pop Idol* Germany. It looks like the waxwork models of two '80s footballers have come alive. '**And the winner is ... Jurgen!**' a woman announces to Gustav's apparent despair.

'This has been a huge number one in Germany,' Foxy is earnestly explaining to Fern and Philip, 'they both did well. Jurgen won. Gustav was second.'

Backstage we see Jurgen eating a bowl of German cabbage.

'I cannot believe I came **second** in the German *Pop Idol*!' Gustav despairs.

'**Sauerkraut?**' Jurgan offers him.

'**I know!**' weeps Gustav.

Meanwhile Foxy, who's in on the joke, is proving himself to be an expert liar, '**They've done their solo records,**' he tells a

Ant's laughable Dr Fox mask fools no one.

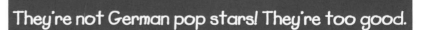
They're not German pop stars! They're too good.

somewhat dubious looking Fern and Phllip, **'they've been number one and now they've done a song together, they've done their equivalent of "The Long And Winding Road".'**

'So,' says Philip. **'Over to Jurgen and Gustav with their latest song: "Mein Herz Mit Dich."'**

With much fist clenching, gurning and hair-shaking the two Germans proceed to make Will Young's version of **'Light My Fire'** look understated. Anyone would think that Ant and Dec know a thing or two about being in a bad pop duo!

Diaorrhea

Ant: 'We wanted to do a live TV show and we thought *SMTV* or *cd:uk* would be too obvious because we'd presented them. This Morning just seemed like the obvious one. Of all the characters we've done they were the hardest voices to get right, the ugliest and least believable. It's all about body proportion. When you put the layers on your face it makes your head bigger and then you put a wig on top of your own hair – it actually looked I had elephantiasis. My head was huge! That was why we had to stay away from Philip and Fern. They knew something was up but luckily they didn't know it was us. Since then we've worked out how to improve the costumes.'

Where is the cash ?

Wait till you hear our cover of 'Evergreen'

My heart with you

TCR 19:41:37:00

'We have a message for you, but first, could I have my top lip back, if you don't mind?'

Philip moves closer to the monitor as though he can't believe his eyes, while Fern stands laughing and shaking her head. For the benefit of viewers who can't understand German the lyrics are subtitled:

'I don't understand,' Jurgen croons.
'Will he need an operation? / It stings! / It aches!/
Yeeaaah /
My heart with you /
Diaorrhea! /
Diaorrhea!
Yeeeahh!'

'How much is that?' Gustav joins in in a heartrending baritone.
'Where is the cash? /

That is very expensive / Where is the cash/ I'll come back La-ter! /Yeeahhh! /
My heart with you! /
My heart with you!'

We then cut to Gustav and Jurgen swaggering towards Fern and Philip on the sofa. As they get closer you can see that the two presenters realise there's something very wrong with these 'Germans'.

'We would like to say thank you,' says Jurgen in a bad German accent. 'It has been a pleasure us being on your show.'

'It's a pleasure,' says Fern politely, stifling a giggle.

'And we have a message from some mutual friends, from Ant & Dec,' says Gustav / Dec.

Philip laughs, at last starting to guess what's going on.

'And thank you for appearing on our TV show Saturday Night Take-away' laughs Ant, in his real voice.

'Oh my god!' claps Phil. 'I didn't know it was you! I had no idea.'

(Later) We cut to Gustav and Jurgen sitting backstage again holding two large flasks of beer and humming 'Deutschland Uber Alles'.

'To the top of the chart we shall go!' toasts Jurgen.

'Just seeing Philip Schofield introduce it as "Here they are with Mein Herz Mit Dich was quite fun. And Foxy was really good. I think Philip said something about us being really ugly and he went: "Hey, come on! These guys have feelings!" God bless you Foxy!'

Where is the cash?

My heart with you!

Mein Herz Mit Dich

It stings! It aches!

'Sauerkraut?'

Jurgen

Yeeahhh!

Gustav

The Evil Producer

If you've ever wondered who has the job of tormenting Ant and Dec every week on 'What's Next?' or of working out whether it's really feasible for two Geordie lads to fool people into thinking they're Cockney geriatrics or Jamaican ladies, then meet Nigel Hall, the dark lord of Saturday Night TV…

SO ARE YOU MR SENSIBLE, TELLING ANT AND DEC WHAT THEY CAN OR CAN'T DO AND WHAT IS TECHNICALLY FEASIBLE?

'Up to a point. They're very TV savvy so they kind of know what is achievable but they always like to

push things just a bit harder and they always want to do something that's a bit more daring. They come in here and they've got really, really big ideas and I say, "I don't think you can do that to the Royal Family, Ant"'

WHAT MOST SURPRISED YOU ABOUT THEM?

'I'd thought they were great ever since *Byker Grove* and I always wanted

to work with them. And of course you wonder what they'll be like in real life. Well, it's a horrible cliché but they really are as fantastic and nice and funny in real life as they are on screen. The friendship that they have is like the friendship that everybody should have. **Everyone should have a best friend like Ant or Dec.'**

HAVE YOU EVER ACCIDENTALLY CALLED DEC ANT OR ANT DEC?

'All the time! When we first started working we all used to do that all the time. You do get used to it. And they're so used to it, it's not a problem.'

WHAT'S THE CRAZIEST IDEA THAT THEY, OR ANY OF THE CREW, HAVE COME UP WITH?

'Everything we really wanted to do we've done but there are moments when you think: "Are we going to get away with this?" Like flying the boys all the way to Texas to audition for Simon Cowell. I was spending a fortune and I just thought, "If this goes wrong, if Simon Cowell spots it's them straight away, I've spent all the show's money and it'll be a disaster". I didn't sleep for two nights, and I was desperate for the boys to ring and say, "We've got it". I was actually at the theatre, at the *Rocky Horror Show*, and I'd got my earpiece in from my mobile, and in the middle of the show Ant rang from Texas and I literally stood up in my seat and went, **"Yes! Yes!"**

I ran out of the theatre and I was just dancing in the road and all these people came out at the interval going: "What's the matter?" and I said: **"Watch the telly!! Watch the telly in January!!"** I just thought "I can't remember the last time it was this exciting!'"

IS IT DIFFICULT TO DO THE 'WHAT'S NEXT'S' WITHOUT THEM KNOWING WHAT'S GOING ON?

'Ant and Dec are nosey parkers so to do a part of the show where they have no idea what's happening is a nightmare. They ask everybody on the team: they've tried to bribe people to tell them what it is. We wind them up all week going: "It's really dangerous this time". And they have to have a medical and they're

asking the nurse. They're like kids at Christmas poking all the presents. So far we've got away with it but they're unbelievable.'

HAVE YOU EVER LOOKED AT THE ADS THAT COME UP AND THOUGHT 'OH NO, WE CAN'T AFFORD TO GIVE THAT AWAY!'?

'Our ambition was always that if there are three Barratt homes advertised in the show that we've chosen then we're giving away three Barratt homes. It's never happened but we have given away five cars in

one prize package and some major holidays. They're not provided to us. We pay for all of them.'

WHAT WAS THE IDEA BEHIND 'HOME RUN'? DO YOU REALLY RESENT PEOPLE GOING OUT AND IGNORING YOUR LOVELY TELEVISION PROGRAMME?

'Television never really acknowledges that there's a whole world going on while the show's on. Do people think that the Bingo halls, and pubs, and clubs, and restaurants just stop because the TV's on? Of course not! We decided to acknowledge that world but try and encourage people to leave it and come back and watch the show. How can people go out when we're working on ITV on a

Saturday night? So we just tried to come up with ideas for the funniest places we could visit on a Saturday night to try and persuade people to go home: we did the Bingo hall, the aeroplane, the dog track. When we did the Bingo hall I thought some people wouldn't go home because they've paid their ticket and they'll think: "Do I go home where there might be £3,000, or do I carry on playing Bingo 'cos I might win £50,000 on the national game.'"

After that, things get a little bit twisted. Ant and Dec are strapped down to a table, and the circus chief then slices their shirts open and brings out a huge snake, which he proceeds to drape over their backs. At this point the circus is almost living up to its billing, until, that is, they bring out the lobsters.

You wonder whether there was a production meeting where they decided on what scary creatures to use.

Snakes? Good! **Lizards?** Too unpredictable. **Elephants?** Too large and incontinent. **Crabs?** Too many connotations. **I know! we'll use lobsters!**

They let the scary, scary lobsters have the run of Ant and Dec's backs for a little while but pretty soon the crustaceans are looking rather bored and listless. **'You survived that one,'** observes the chief freak, with some disappointment, but he's got another trick in store. The show finishes with knife-throwers hurling lethally sharp blades just millimetres from Ant and Dec's faces, but that's nothing for two presenters who've just survived the **'Lobsters of Doom.'**

'You're all sacked,' Ant tells the production team charitably as they're at last released.

NO DEC, THIS TIME IT ISN'T A BLOKE IN A SNAKE SUIT

Beware! The lobsters of doom

Ant: 'I hated it! As soon as the curtain went up and all those women dressed in dominatrix gear appeared, which I quite liked actually, and then all the other weird-looking half-dead guys — oh no! If I'd put a top ten list of things I didn't want to be involved in that'd be pretty high up there I think. The audience seemed to love it, though, when the snake went over our backs. People went "Ooh, you looked really scared!" **Well, of course I was!** The feller had ripped me t-shirt open with a knife, or a pair of scissors or something, and there was a ten foot python on my back.'

Dec: '**Then they put lobsters on our back!** Apparently they had the lobsters' claws fixed with elastic bands but **there was a guy behind us nipping me back to make it feel like it was the lobsters.** We just didn't know what was going to happen.'

Win the Ads 1

Ant and Dec are very impressionable and often go and buy things they've just seen on the telly. Apparently, though, some people aren't that impressionable and don't rush out to buy four TVs, two lawn mowers and softener that makes your clothes easier to iron. So, to help these people, they invented 'Don't Just Watch The Ads, Win Them' See how you'd get on...

1 Who was crowned 'King Of The Jungle' in May?
a   John Fashanu
b   Phil Tufnell

2 Whose birthday party did Aaron Barschak crash?
a   Prince William
b   The Queen

3 What was the title of the fifth Harry Potter book?
a   *Harry Potter and the Order Of The Phoenix*
b   *Harry Potter and the Goblet Of Doom*

4 What did pop duo Jemini become famous for this year?
a   Receiving 'nil points' at the Eurovision song contest?
b   Topping the charts in every European country but the UK?

5 At which ageing star's Barbados home did Tony Blair spend his summer holiday?
a   Ozzy Osbourne
b   Cliff Richard

6 What shirt number did David Beckham agree to wear when he moved to Real Madrid?
a   twenty three
b   seven

7 Which critically-panned film did J-Lo and Ben Affleck star in?
a   *Gigli*
b   *Dumb and Dumberer*

8 Who sang 'Sound Of The Underground'?
a   Girls Aloud
b   tATU

9 Who won the Wimbledon Men's Tennis Championship?
a   Andy Roddick
b   Roger Federer

10 Which Hollywood star announced that he was going into politics?
a   Bruce Willis
b   Arnold Schwarzenegger

14 Which 80s popstar sat alongside Simon Cowell on *American Idol*?
a Paula Abdul
b Debbie Gibson

15 What were the names of the characters Ant and Dec played in *Byker Grove*?
a Robson and Jerome
b PJ and Duncan

16 Which comedy legend died at the age of a hundred in 2003?
a Bob Hope
b George Burns

11 Which football team did Russian oil billionaire Roman Abramovich turn into the money-bags of Europe?
a Chelsea
b Real Madrid

17 Who or what achieved a record speed of 208mph?
a Michael Schumacher in practise for the Monaco Grand Prix
b The Eurostar train on the way through Kent

12 Who sang 'The Fast Food Song'
a The Fast Food Rockers
b The Fast Food Freaks

18 Who said, 'I'm just a bit giddy with my own success at the minute. I mean that in a really humble way.'
a Tony Blair
b Robbie Williams

13 What anniversary did The Oscars celebrate this year?
a 50th
b 75th

19 Who met a watery end in *Coronation Street*?
a Peter Barlow
b Tricky Dicky

20 What animal was cloned for the first time in August this year?
a a goat
b a horse

Pop stars

Ant and Dec had some of the biggest stars in the world come and join them on *Saturday Night Takeaway*. Some of them probably thought that they were just going to sing their latest hit, nick some hospitality booze and leave. It's to their credit that when they found out they were expected to face surreal interrogation from Little Ant and Dec or a series of ridiculous sketches, that most of them stuck around anyway. . .

The Great Tom Jones – the former PJ and Duncan are not worthy.

Mariah Carey insisted on getting to perform some magic when she appeared on the show. She waved her magic wand and turned Ant and Dec into rabbits.

When they first saw the Liberty X girls Ant and Dec probably thought it was the scary PVC girls from the circus coming back for more. Until, that is, they realised that the janitors practising their off-side trap behind them were actually the Liberty X boys.

Kym Marsh's biggest ambition as a child was to sing with the Bangles. And come to think of it, she does bear a spooky resemblance to Susanna Hoffs. Next time she comes we'll give her a 'Little Susanna' label.

Darius was very keen to get involved in the programme, even volunteering to go undercover with this cunning disguise. Unfortunately Ant and Dec aren't that easy to fool, as any one who saw the 'Gorillas' episode will know.

World-conquering pop sensation Justin Timberlake took time out to pay a visit to the *Saturday Night Takeaway* stage door. But no dressing-room demands for him – Ant and Dec sent him straight out again to buy the prizes for the show.

Undercover
American Idol

Paula is impressed with Scotty and Jimmy.

It's the last day of the **American Idol** heats in Austin, Texas. Two wannabe rock dudes with tattoos, lank hair and 'street' clothes are hanging out in the lobby waiting for their audition with **Simon Cowell, '80s popstar Paula Abdul and producer Randy Jackson.**

'Jimmy' is practising his break-dancing on the carpeted floor, 'Scotty' is doing a sort of pointy-elbowed dance that makes him look like he's trying to clear a space for himself at the New Year sales. You wouldn't put money on either of them to make it to the final in Hollywood, until, that is, another (genuine) hopeful shows off a few of his own moves. He dances, like a librarian with an artificial hip, and suddenly Jimmy and Scotty look like real contenders.

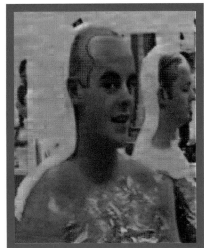

Unfortunately, when Jimmy gets called in front of the terrible trio, his nerve deserts him. **'I'm sorry,'** he mutters, apparently tongue-tied.

As you'd expect, Simon shows him all the patience and encouragement that he's famous for, sighing heavily and staring blankly into the middle distance.

'Bring your brother in,' Paula suggests.

With the arrival of Scotty, things immediately improve. 'What song are you going to do?' Paula asks.

'Opposites Attract', Jimmy answers. Simon's face doesn't change. It's hard to tell whether he thinks performing a song written by one of the judges (Paula) is a cheesy idea.

Has little *Jimmy* got what it takes?

Or whether he thinks two brothers singing a duet that was originally about fancying your co-vocalist is a bit, um, weird.

Of course, Jimmy and Scotty are edgy, rocking, hip-hop dudes so their version starts with an alarming rap from Jimmy and features customised lyrics 'Who woulda thought / we could be brothers' (do you see what they've done there?). Simon is gazing at them with an expression of mild bemusement as though he's sure he's seen them somewhere before but can't quite place them.

The song finishes with some trademark break-dancing from Jimmy (the dying fish, I think that manoeuvre's called) and human

beatboxing from Scotty and, shock, Simon is actually smiling. He knows something's up. Probably because these guys are actually so much more professional than most of the performers he's seen.

'Do you think if we can't make it as popstars we could be presenters?' asks Scotty.

'Maybe if we stood like this,' says Jimmy moving to stand on the other side of the stage.

'And spoke a bit more Geordie, like this?' laughs Scotty aka Ant returning to his natural accent.

'You!' Simon waggles his finger at them. For once he's almost speechless. You can tell how shocked

he is. He even says something nice.

'This was not an unusual performance!' he laughs. **'This was a good one!'**

Dec: 'We went out there and before going on we decided to immerse ourselves in American culture so we went to Wal-Mart and walked around and it went really well. We talked to shop assistants and bought stuff and got a cab back to the hotel and the cab driver said "Why are you guys here?" and we said "We're here to audition for American Idol" and he said: "Oh yeah man, Simon Cowell, blah, blah, blah," and we thought "Yeah! We're pulling it off, we've got the American accents, we look like a couple of American kids, brilliant!" Then we pulled up at the hotel and the guy said: "So, where you guys from in England?" Ha! Shattered confidence!'

Dec: 'The night before we flew to Texas, I got a phone call from Nigel, the executive producer, saying: "Have a good time out there, don't worry about it 'cos it's cost a lot of money, there's no pressure, but if you don't pull it off, you're sacked!"'

Ant: "I was standing in the queue thinking: "I stand out like a sore thumb. I'm an English guy with an American accent. I've got a wig on, I've got a tattoo up my neck, I've got an earring." Then I looked and the guy after me was dressed like a wizard and I thought: "Actually, I might get away with this.""

Little Simon wants to know if you have to wear these clothes to be properly nasty. Couldn't he be nasty with the waistband slightly lower?

WHAT'S NEXT? ??

COUNTDOWN

When Ant and Dec came up with 'What's Next?' it seemed like a brilliant idea. They'd leave the production crew to do all the work sorting out that segment of the show while they took the afternoon off.

When they stood by the curtain for the first time, though, having no idea what was behind it, they must have wondered if it was quite such a good scheme after all.

But, if they were taking it easy, the production team were proving that they could take it easier still. For the first ever 'What's Next?' they just borrowed the set of *Countdown*, complete with presenters Richard Whiteley and Carol Vorderman and let them do all the work. To begin with, you might have thought that this was going to be a joke edition of the programme. But no: the ties are wacky, the puns are terrible and the quiz is fiendishly difficult and addictive. For the next ten minutes this *is* *Countdown*. To add to the sense that we're in a world that hasn't changed since 1984, they've even managed to track down Ant's old headteacher Mrs Sheila Clement-Jones.

ANTHONY & DECLAN

STARRING CAROL FOUR DOOR VAN

Anthony McPartlin aged 27. He says he's an entertainer from Newcastle on Tyne. He loves show jumping and stamp collecting. So tonight he hopes to be riding high and telling his opponent to stick it.

'We always knew he had something about him,' she reminisces fondly as she looks at Ant. 'Not sure what.'

'Must have been the high forehead,' Ant splutters, trying to retain his cool, but you can tell he feels about twelve years old again, 'no brain in there, but it's very high.'

'Have you played Countdown before?' Richard asks.

'Only at home,' says Dec. 'I'm good at home.'

'Not in the studio eh?' says Richard helpfully. 'You'll be a bit nervous I expect, with all the lights and people and everything, and the fact that it's live.'

'Yes, exactly – thanks Richard,' says Ant dryly.

Meanwhile Dec's pen is whirling agitatedly through his fingers as he gazes at Carol. This is obviously a moment he's dreamt about many times before. 'A vowel please, Carol,' he asks seductively.

'A vowel?' she responds, sounding strangely astonished considering this is about the thousandth time she's done this job.

Declan Donnely aged 27 from Newcastle. He says he's just as entertaining as Anthony – his hobby is helping his mother bake cakes so tonight he's hoping to be the cherry on the top.

STARRING RICHARD WHITE TEETH

I'm Very Very HAPPY

I Y E N G R A T D

When all nine letters are up, and the famous musical timer starts, Dec begins dancing in his seat, receiving a disapproving glance from Mrs C-J. If it had been Ant, no doubt she'd have had something to say about it. Although perhaps if she'd clamped down more severely on showing-off he might not be here now.

As expected the head gets a better word G R A T I N G than A+D – 'grating' to their 'grated' but, shockingly, she's made a mistake. There's only one 'g' but she's used it twice. 'See', thinks Ant, 'it's not my fault that I ended up here. It's my teacher's'.

T H A D N I W E S

Things go from bad to worse in the numbers round where they all get their sums completely wrong. They've only got the Countdown Conundrum to save face: 'T-H-A-D-N-I-W-E-S'. Luckily for Mrs C-J she gets it within a few seconds. **'Win The Ads!'** she triumphs, and the reputation of her school, if not that of one of her pupils, is saved.

W I N T H E A D S

Dec: 'I really enjoyed Countdown. I play it at home, well, everyone plays it at home, don't they? But I pretend that I'm not really playing it 'cos I can never get more than four letters. When the screen came down I thought: "Oh, this is gonna be easy, me playing against Ant at Countdown – I'm easily gonna win! Hahahaha!" Then Ant's old headmistress came down and I thought: "We're never gonna beat a teacher!" But it was great, being on the Countdown set with Richard and Carol.'

Dec: 'I thought I had the numbers game cracked but I used my 10 twice. A schoolboy error. To this day, I regret that.'

Ant: 'That "do-da-do-do" goes a lot faster when you're trying to think of something in the studio, I can tell you. You just end up singing along to the tune in your head.'

Mr and Mesmerised

Caroline Brooks didn't think anything of it when Dec clambered into the audience and asked her if she remembered the old TV show *Mr And Mrs*. Her husband was just running a bit late wasn't he? Um, no. Like the mad scientists of light entertainment that they are, Ant and Dec had created a weird hybrid of *Mr and Mrs* and a hypnosis roadshow and her husband, Martin, was to be the first victim, erm, contestant.

Dec: 'I loved 'Mr and Mesmerised'. We hypnotised quite a few people and some people had trouble going under, or they were so under that they were really boring, but we hit on this one guy who was great and his wife was tremendous. You could see how scared he was because he'd got no idea what he'd said!'

Ant: 'It turned out OK, though, because she got a lot of prizes so she wasn't too angry!'

'It's dead easy,' Dec lies. 'Question one is for his-and-hers matching bath-robes. First of all we asked Martin: Which TV personality does your mother-in-law remind you of? Now, did Martin say, a: Janice Battersby, b: Lily Savage, or did he say, c: Something else? What do you think?'

Caroline is bemused. 'Do you know?' she asks Martin, who has now joined her down on the 'Mr and Mesmerised' set.

'No I don't remember!' says Martin, shrinking into his chair and wondering what he's got himself into.

'Oh,' says Caroline, presumably thinking that he must have thought of someone a bit more acceptable than either 'a' or 'b'. 'Someone else I hope!'

'Well let's find out,' says Dec turning to the monitor where we see Martin stretched out in the couch earlier in the day.

'What TV personality does your mother in law remind you of?' the hypnotist asks the prone Martin gently.

Martin has no trouble coming up with an answer. 'On telly? Erm, *Coronation Street*, "I say", **Fred Elliot.'**

Oh!

Caroline laughs and shakes her head. **'She'll kill you!'** she promises.

'Question two,' begins Ant, 'for Champagne and bubble bath! We asked Martin: **'has your wife got any bad habits?** Did he say, a: she snores, b: she breaks wind a lot, or c: something else. What do you reckon?'

'I snore,' admits Caroline fairly confidently.

'She snores a lot,' Martin frowns on the screen, masochistically determined to answer this one as fully as possible. 'In bed, heavy. Sometimes she sucks flannels. She chews on flannels,' he demonstrates with a disturbing chomping noise like an old man who's lost his false teeth.

'Only when I'm pregnant!' Caroline protests.

'Question three,' Dec asks. 'This is for a tea's-made! For anyone under thirty that's an alarm clock and kettle in one! Brilliant!' Dec pretends to be joking but you can tell he's genuinely impressed by the idea. 'We asked Martin: **'do you think any of your wife's friends fancy you?''**

Martin puts his head in his hands watching his marriage crumble through his fingers.

'Did he say,' Dec continues regardless. 'a: I think Julia does, b: they all do, or did he say c: something else?'

'They all do, knowing him' replies the long-suffering Caroline.

'Yeah, I think they all do!' says Martin matter-of-factly, hardly even seeming to be hypnotised.

'So far you have won all the prizes,' Ant promises. 'Final question. Who does your wife fancy on television? Did Martin say a: Robson Green, b: Nick Berry or c: someone else?

Caroline seems pretty sure she knows the answer. 'Someone else,' she smiles, just slightly embarrassed.

'She fancies Ant & Dec,' Martin answers without jealousy. "Ooh, her boys', she says 'my boys!"

Ant and Dec are practically preening. **'I'm very, very flattered indeed!'** Ant laughs. 'And I tell you what, you've won every prize, you two know each other inside out! Well done!'

As one last bonus prize they even let Martin decide what extra prize Caroline would like. Under hypnosis of course.

'If you could give your wife a real treat what would it be?'

'I think my wife would like to be pampered. With a show, or

hotel, health farm,' he answers, at once saving his marriage.

Caroline is genuinely touched and a little bit teary-eyed but Ant and Dec have got one more surprise for them. All the way from Alicante in Spain Caroline's mother, Sheila, arrives, dressed, inevitably as Fred Elliot from *Coronation Street*.

'Why do you think he called you Fred Elliot!' Ant asks but Sheila doesn't seem to know.

'I'll kill him I say, I say I'll kill him!' she laughs.

Dec: 'We've got the board game, 'Mr And Mrs', at home and we play it with our girlfriends and, obviously, always get the answers horribly wrong. I always thought it was a great idea and doing it under hypnotism is a great twist. We want to do more of that kind of thing – just fun with hypnotism. I want to do "He's got your willy and you really want it back!" That's genius!'

39

Little People

Big Ant and Dec were supposed to write this bit but they couldn't be bothered. We do all the hardest jobs on 'Saturday Night Takeaway' and here are some pictures of us holding Kylie's knickers to prove it . . .

Big Ant and Dec don't throw underwear at stars.

We do. And Kylie thought we were sweet!

So that's when we told her our 'girls' joke!

40

We like Little Simon Cowell, but we think big Simon Cowell is distinctly average.

Little Darius says he can feel the love in the room but we think it's probably just something he ate.

41

Little People

After we appeared on 'Saturday Night Takeaway' all the stars wanted a Little version of themselves. All of them, that is, except Will Young. For some reason he insisted that he didn't have a Little Will...

Little Lorraine Kelly pretends she doesn't like us.

But we don't think she'll start an 'I hate boys' club.

Girls love little Tom Jones. He gets underwear thrown at him too.

42

But we've had enough of all that.

Little little Ant and Dec... don't know how hard this job is.

But we think they'll want to join the 'we hate girls' club.

'This is the way you'll be when your old'

Suddenly the link goes dead. Lorraine turns to the girls with a mixture of amusement and concern, **'Oh no, I've got a horrible feeling there was a ring involved!'** she says.

Meanwhile Kenny and George are using that fortuitous technical hitch to get from Southend to London in record time. When the live link reappears, all that Lorraine and the *GMTV* viewers see is Kenny's dog, sitting in his wheelchair, barking his head off.

'Oh no,' says Lorraine again, suddenly realising that she might have been set-up. **'There's something going on here!'**

Kenny and George AKA Ant and Dec lurch towards her, but by now the canny presenter has worked out who it is. **'It's you two!'** she cries. **'You, you. . .'** If you watch very carefully you can see her mouth the word 'b****rs!' live on breakfast television.

As usual, though, Lorraine isn't fazed for long. When Kenny and George ask her to marry them instead of the waiting actresses she happily accepts both offers. **'Look at you two,'** she laughs, even managing to get her own back just a little bit, **'this is the way you'll look when you're old!'**

'Oh, no . . . there's something going on here . . .'

Ant: 'She's been doing the show for years and years and we thought if anyone's going to catch us it'll be her. She could quite easily have gone: "Hi Ant and Dec" and that would have ruined the whole thing. Going into that one I was probably the most nervous I've been. But the girls were tremendous. They didn't look too bimbo-ish like a page 3 model or something. They were just normal, pretty girls.'

Dec: 'Lorraine was expecting them to be a bit harder, tattooed, the girl you'd find in the local chippy. She was planning to nail these girls as being gold-diggers. We were really looking forward to it. We didn't know any of the questions she was going to ask so we just had to play it by ear. When she asked: "Is there a sexual side to the relationship"... Ha! I really hoped that she'd ask that question.'

Win the Ads 2

Don't Just Watch The Ads, Win Them!

There's nothing like being generous with someone else's money. That's why Ant and Dec would like to let you have the opportunity to win the entire contents of the ads shown during last year's *Saturday Night Takeaway*. They'd like to, but they can't. The publishers of this book aren't that generous. Still, have a go and see how you'd fare if this was the real thing...

1 Which Simpsons character dubbed the French 'cheese-eating surrender monkeys'?
a Homer
b Grounds-Keeper Willy

2 Which '80s pop band reformed this year?
a Duran Duran
b Wham!

3 What did fashion experts decide was back in this summer?
a Moustaches
b Cowboy boots

4 What world record did Tanya Streeter break this year?
a Deepest dive without oxygen
b Loudest scream

5 Who won the Community Shield football match at the start of the 2003/2004 season?
a Arsenal
b Manchester United

6 Which new rock band features the Hawkins brothers?
a The Strokes
b The Darkness

7 What Beatles' song did Cherie Blair serenade Chinese students with?
a 'When I'm 64'
b 'Yellow Submarine'

8 On which TV show did Aggie and Kim appear?
a *The Dinner Party Inspectors*
b *How Clean Is Your House?*

9 Which band followed Abba and Queen in having a musical based on their songs?
a Madness
b Spandau Ballet

10 Which former game-show host is now behind the bar at The Vic?
a Shane Ritchie
b Les Dennis

11 Who left *Emmerdale* to look for treasure in South America?
a Zac Dingle
b Seth Armstrong

12 What programme did *Big Brother 3* winner Kate Lawler end up presenting?
a *RI:SE*
b *GMTV*

13 Who headlined the Glastonbury Festival 2003 on Saturday night?
a David Bowie
b Radiohead

14 Who played Bill The Butcher in Martin Scorsese's *Gangs Of New York*?
a Leonardo DiCaprio
b Daniel Day-Lewis

15 Which pop band disbanded first?
a S-Club 7
b 5ive

16 Who was voted off *Big Brother 4* first?
a Anoushka
b Lisa

17 Which former Heavyweight Champion of the World was declared bankrupt after blowing over $500 million?
a Mike Tyson
b Rocky Marciano

18 Oasis frontman Liam Gallagher lost what in a confrontation with Italian youths?
a his front teeth
b the masters of the latest Oasis album

19 Who played Adam Sandler's therapist in *Anger Management*?
a Jim Carrey
b Jack Nicholson

20 A new record high temperature was set in August this year but what was the old record?
a 37.1 centigrade
b 42.5 centigrade

WHAT'S NEXT? ??? ?

If the producers judge 'What's Next?' by how successfully they manage to put Ant and Dec through the wringer then this week's must have been one of their favourites. It starts with them changing into full navy uniform, complete with ever so slightly flared white trousers, and joining a group of fit, athletic sailors for one of those exercise routines that our Armed Forces do to prove to people that there's absolutely nothing camp about a group of men together at sea. Certainly not.

NAVY

Dec: 'I quite enjoyed the navy one but it was extremely energetic. I was sweating at the end of it. There was a lot of falling over. I tripped over me log at one point.'

Ant: 'Did you have trouble with your log?'

Dec: 'I did have trouble with me log. It was good fun but it seemed to go on for ages and I was knackered.'

Cue the Village People's 'In The Navy', then, and in run a group of young men (and alright a couple of young women, too) holding a large, polished tree trunk between their legs which they proceed to leap backwards and forwards over. At this point Dec must be wondering whether Ant knows something he doesn't. Somehow, while the former is sandwiched between two strapping blokes who are at least a head taller than him, Ant seems to have mysteriously found himself next to the only Wrens. This means that when the sailors raise the log above their heads, Ant can just about hang on on tip-toes but Dec is lifted right off the ground.

Good, clean, innocent fun

They're then made to jump over the log held just a few feet in the air, a task which is like jumping an ant-hill for the sailors, like jumping Mount Everest for the short-arsed Geordies. By now you can see that Ant and Dec think that they've got the idea but there's one more punishment waiting. Two of the sailors drop down, with their ankles locked over the log, and begin doing press-ups. 'There's no way I can do that!' Ant and Dec think to themselves and they're right. They try to throw themselves down with some enthusiasm but have a little bit of trouble with the pushing-themselves-back-up bit.

Luckily the finale is a lot easier. They're hoisted triumphantly into the air by the sailors like a couple of kitbags. They look at each other wryly as the audience cheer. Whose idea was 'What's Next?' again?

"jump over the log!"

Dec: 'We had a guy behind us whispering instructions in our ear.'

Ant: 'I had a girl, actually. I quite enjoyed that …'

Dec: 'Every now and then they'd be going "hold on to the log!" And next thing I knew I'd be up in the air. Then he says "jump over the log!" and the other bloke's shouting "don't jump over your log!" (cries) "But he told me to jump over my log!"'

"Don't jump over your log!"

Undercover
Fortune Tellers

Peter Ogden never believed in Fortune Tellers. The only reason he went to see Patti and Bernice, a pair of, shall we say, idiosyncratic, Jamaican psychics was to prove to his friends that it's all rubbish. Luckily he's a polite, well-brought up chap because Patti and Bernice's methods are a little bit, um, unusual. The first thing they ask him to do is to put on a kind of turban-style hat, with little sparkly bits on the front. 'We're from Jamaica and we do things a little different there,' Bernice explains, as though ridiculous 'Arabian Nights'-style hats are all the rage in the Caribbean.

You can see Peter relax as he decides that his beliefs about fortune tellers are completely justified. It probably doesn't help that Patti and Bernice's fortune-telling booth seems to have been furnished from 'Charlatans R Us' with a plasticky crystal ball and over-sized candles. Then suddenly the two psychics start making some eerily accurate guesses about his life.

'Are you originally from an island?' Bernice asks.

'Yes,' he admits, a little surprised.

'So are we,' says Patti.

'Jamaica,' nods Peter.

'Yours is a smaller island than that, though, isn't it?' says Bernice staring deep into the crystal ball.

'Island....Island.... Island of Man?'

Peter is stunned.

'Is that true?'

'Yeah!'

'You have three brothers?'

'Yes!'

'One sister?'

Peter doesn't know what to think now. 'How do you know this?'

'You can tell in the crystal ball,' Bernice explains.

They then persuade him to take off his shoes and socks and press his feet against the crystal ball.

'In the Caribbean we don't read the palm, we read the. . .sole!' Patti explains with a straight face.

THE HERMIT

THE HIGH PRIESTESS

JUSTICE

'I think we need to give him some good luck,' says Patti, the second time.

'Bring in the snake!'

Peter practically jumps out of his chair. 'Noooo,' he shudders, his arms wind-milling as though invisible snakes are swirling around him. 'Woah! I hate snakes.'

'Come on man, it's OK,' says Bernice calmly. 'He's just a snake.'

Peter's eyes widen and he jumps out of his skin again. 'No, No!'

'All you have to do is put your hand in to this trunk and stroke the snake,' says Bernice cajolingly.

'No way!' says Peter, his hands fiddling nervously with his ridiculous hat as he runs for the door.

'I see a lot of good things,' Bernice says thoughtfully. 'A lot of trouble. And I also see love.'

'Who with?' asks Peter, perking up slightly.

'With a woman,' says Bernice, not particularly narrowing things down, although Peter would probably be

glad to know that Patti and Bernice are both ruled out.

Unfortunately, when Patti begins dealing the tarot cards the death card comes up, twice.

'That can sometimes mean change,' says Bernice, the first time.

Luckily for him the snake seems to have escaped and the two psychics seem fairly confident that it escaped before they arrived in their booth. Peter relaxes a little bit.

'Let's play some music and I will find your aura,' Bernice decides.

'Just move around, that's it,' encourages Bernice, grinding her broad body. 'Shimmy down and move your hips.'

Unwisely Peter copies her, even though if Bernice's dancing reveals any aura it's that of your dad at the Christmas party.

Peter frowns but looks intrigued.

'You going to meet someone famous,' says Bernice, grabbing Peter's wrist. 'In fact, you are going to meet someone famous right now. And that person is...' he gives up the Jamaican accent.

Ant: 'We lost it by the end. I was saying "Dance, dance around your aura, scream" and he went "Yeah!" and I said "Louder" and he said "Yeah!" and Dec was cracking up!'

'This has been a stressful time,' she says soothingly as though the stress had nothing to do with her and Patti.

The music starts and Bernice begins to dance. 'You may need to move to release the aura.' She explains.

'OK,' he sighs, beginning to sway backwards and forwards.

'Move back and forward, back and forward. Give me a scream.' Bernice encourages.

'Yeah!' croaks Peter.

'Give me another scream,' says Bernice

'Yeah, yeah!' says Peter, starting to get into the spirit of it now.

'I can see your aura. I can tell you going to be on TV,' says Patti.

'Me, Ant!'

Peter almost collapses with laughter.

'And me Dec!'

'This is *Saturday Night Takeaway!*' Ant laughs. 'What have you got to say?'

'Oh my God!' says Peter, suddenly realising that he might look a little bit silly. 'I'm really glad I'm wearing this hat!'

Dec: 'We did quite a lot of people on the fortune tellers one. I think we saw about seven people and they were OK but it wasn't quite working. That's the thing with "Undercover" – there are no guaranteed results, but then suddenly this guy walks in...'

Ant: 'We knew a friend of his who set him up and gave us all this information about his family and friends and stuff like that. So we started dropping all these things in and he was really, really shocked. His face just went like that (open-mouthed). "How did you know that? How did you know that?" (Patti accent) "Because we're fortune tellers and we see it all in the crystal ball". And because he was so scared of snakes he was ready to run out the door in his bare feet with a turban on his head! He was funny. A good guy.'

Patti and Bernice's
Predictions for 2004...

LIONEL

FOOTBALL: The European Championships

Patti: 'We'd need to read David Beckham's feet to tell you about that.'

Bernice: 'Yes, we want to let his feet do the talking.'

Patti: 'I'd let the rest of him do the talking, too!'

GUSTAV AND JURGEN

Patti: 'The tarot card says death'

Bernice: 'But that can just mean change.'

Patti: 'Yes, I see a split over musical differences. Gustav wants them to sound like David Hasselhoff's first album but Jurgen is angry. He says David Hasselhoff's second album is much better.'

KENNY AND GEORGE

Bernice: 'The tarot card says death.'

Patti: 'But that can just mean change.'

Bernice: 'And it can just mean death.'

ANT AND DEC

Patti: 'I see a drama series for children, set in Newcastle, and then a very successful pop career.'

Bernice: 'Patti! You've got the crystal ball upside down!'

REALITY TV

Bernice: 'There's a big star, an enormous star, going into the jungle to perform terrible tasks. It's not, it's not Tony Blair is it!?'

Patti: 'Or is that Lionel Blair?'

Bernice: 'It's one of the two.'

POP MUSIC

Patti: 'I see a big comeback for PJ and Duncan.'

Bernice: 'Unless everybody keeps watching Ant and Dec on telly.'

Patti: 'So please, everybody, you have to watch the new series of *Saturday Night Takeaway!!*'

LITTLE ANT AND DEC

Patti: 'Girls, so many girls!'

Bernice: 'I thought they didn't like girls?'

Patti: 'Girls seem to like them.'

POLITICS

Bernice: 'A new Prime Minister will be elected by a programme called *Politics Idol*.

Patti: 'Simon Cowell will be the new Jeremy Paxman.'

Bernice: 'No Jeremy Paxman will be the new Simon Cowell!'

SATURDAY NIGHT TAKEAWAY

Bernice: 'I predict a bright future for *Patti and Bernice's Saturday Night Takeaway*.'

Patti: 'Just as long as they get the name right this time.'

BILL AND BEN

By this weeks 'Whats Next?' the producers realised that they'd put the boot in to Ant and Dec a few too many times. They'd been inconsiderate. It was time to let someone else have a go at putting the boot into them, too. When the curtain opened the first thing the two Geordies saw was the beaming face of their old friend John Thomson. He looked like someone preparing to thoroughly enjoy himself.

'This is the magical world of Bill and Ben the Flower Pot Men,' he announces with an evil grin, 'and here's Jane to tell you your task for tonight.'

If they'd just looked around Ant and Dec should have been able to guess what their task would be. The set behind the curtain is decorated in the ludicrously bright colours that you only ever see on Children's TV (Ikea haven't started a psychedelic toddler vomit range, yet) and there are two, ominously empty, giant flower pots awaiting their occupants. Oh, and Jane Danson, the former *Coronation Street* actress, there to give them their instructions, is dressed as a giant sunflower – aka Weed.

Bright Colours and ridiculous costumes...

Wait till you see your costumes!'

This never happened to the old narrator!

'Hahaha!' they laugh at her.

Strangely, she doesn't seem that bothered by their laughter. 'Wait till you see your costumes!' she grins smugly.

After the break, they come back with mini-flower pots on their heads and giant flower pots around their waists. Their instructions can be summarised as 'do whatever John tells you until he decides he's had enough'.

'Ben was full of the joys of spring and merrily skipped around the garden,' John smirks. 'Come on Ben, skippity-skip!'

'Which one am I?' frowns Ant, as though it's not obvious who is Bill and who is Ben (the original Bill and Ben were pioneers of Ant and Dec's memory-assisting trick – Bill is always on the left of your screen, Ben on the right).

Ant: 'John's face when he saw us was like: "Ahh! I've got you!" We know John, we've known him for a while, and he is a really good laugh. You can tell he'd been waiting to get us. I said afterwards "How long have you been waiting to do this?" and he said "I came in this morning before you got here, before 11, and I've been stuck in the dressing room all day. I felt like Anne Frank stuck in the attic!"'

63

'The Flower Pot Men scratched their heads and wondered what to have for breakfast,' John continued. 'Suddenly they spotted some juicy red apples hanging from the branches of a tree.'

Ant and Dec suddenly realise that this 'What's Next?' actually has a plot of sorts, although, to be fair to them, it's more complex and emotionally involving than anything they did in *Byker Grove*. The first twist comes when, their hunger unsatisfied by the apples, they try and pull a giant carrot out of the ground.

'But the carrot wouldn't budge,' John narrates. 'Ben laughed and said that Bill was as weak as a girl.'

'Flobberlobbergirly!'

Dec improvises brilliantly.

'Bill says that Ben should help him pull the carrot,' John continues. 'So Ben held Bill around his middle and they both pulled with all their might.' The two of them then decide that this is a tale of triumph over adversity so they genuinely pull as hard as they can, determined not to be beaten by the giant plastic vegetable. It comes flying out of the ground and they go flying backwards.

'The carrot wasn't supposed to budge!' John cracks up, in his non-narrator voice.

Um, the script says 'they cower in terror', guys!

Dec: 'We didn't know what to do. We had to listen to John's voice-over to see what we had to do next. He was going "pull the carrot up" but it wasn't moving. He went: "and they pulled again" and we thought "Obviously the carrot's got to come up" so we just looked at each other and went "Let's get this carrot up!" so the carrot comes flying out of the, pot and the floor manager shouted from across the studio "The carrot's not supposed to come up!"'

A flowerpot each? What luxury!

In the next exciting twist they manage to bring down some of the plastic apples with a well-flung plastic marrow, but, before they get the chance to eat them they're (literally) buzzed by a giant wasp. It's Jane's chance to make good all the promise she showed at drama school. 'C'mon wasp, make my day,' she snarls, brandishing an enormous can of insect repellent.

If that wasn't enough it suddenly begins to snow and John takes the opportunity to bring an ecological message into proceedings. 'That's climate change for you,' he intones. 'Brought on by excessive production of greenhouse gases.' Typically, though, its just an excuse for a cheap fart noise gag.

'Oh no! The gardener had woken up and was coming up the garden path,' he finishes, probably determined to bring proceedings to a halt any way he can. Adding to the hilarity, Ant can't get back into his flowerpot. For a second he looks genuinely worried, scrabbling desperately against it.

'Go in that one,' Jane advises him, pointing to Dec's pot.

They both look like their contract specifies separate flowerpots but there isn't much time and they scramble inside.

'Goodnight Weed,' says John still laughing. 'Goodnight Bill, Goodnight Ben.'

Win the Ads 3

Don't Just Watch The Ads, Win Them!

Saturday Night Takeaway's Executive Producer Nigel Hall lives in fear that one day there'll be a South Pacific island advertised in the middle of *Emmerdale*. Try imagining that's what's on offer here, you're standing in the spotlight in front of a hushed audience, and Ant and Dec are rattling through these questions and maybe they won't seem quite so easy ...

1 Who co-hosted ITV2's coverage of *I'm A Celebrity...Get Me Out Of Here!* with Tara Palmer Tompkinson
  a Mark Durden-Smith
  b Michael Parkinson

2 Who had a quick fondle of Kylie while duetting with her at the Brit Awards?
  a Robbie Williams
  b Justin Timberlake

3 What rank had the *Who Wants To Be A Millionaire?* cheat reached in the army?
  a Colonel
  b Major

4 Who were England playing when Wayne Rooney made his debut?
  a Australia
  b Holland

5 What did Stephen Fry tell Little Ant and Dec he would do if caught short at the Baftas?
  a go behind a pot plant
  b go where he was standing and let it run off the stage

6 Who did Lennox Lewis fight in June 2003 to retain his heavyweight title?
  a Vitali Klitschko
  b Oliver McCall

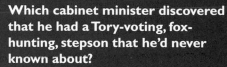

7 What Take That song did Mark Owen duet with Robbie Williams at Knebworth?
a 'Babe'
b 'Back For Good'

8 Which pop princess toured with Justin Timberlake this year?
a Christina Aguilera
b Avril Lavigne

9 What are the Cheeky Girls real names?
a Rosa and Leia
b Monica and Gabriela

10 Who was reported to be richer than the Queen?
a JK Rowling
b David Beckham

11 Who directed *The Hulk*?
a Ang Lee
b Francis Ford Coppola

12 In which soap did Boy George make a guest appearance?
a *Hollyoaks*
b *EastEnders*

13 How long did Jeffrey Archer spend in prison?
a Eighteen months
b Two years

14 Which cabinet minister discovered that he had a Tory-voting, fox-hunting, stepson that he'd never known about?
a Gordon Brown
b John Prescott

15 How much did it cost per day to drive into central London during peak hours, after Ken Livingstone introduced the congestion charge?
a £5
b £10

16 Where is this year's Big Brother winner Cameron from?
a The Orkneys
b The Shetlands

17 Who played Bosley in the first Charlies Angels film
a Samuel L Jackson
b Bill Murray

18 What chart-topping song does the following line come from 'Mother looking at me /Tell me what do you see? /Yes, I've lost my mind'
a tATU's 'All The Things She Said'
b Evanescence's 'Bring Me To Life'

19 Which British city was declared 'European City Of Culture' for 2008
a Liverpool
b Newcastle

20 Who preceded Michael Vaughn as captain of the England Cricket Team?
a Nasser Hussain
b Michael Atherton

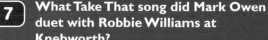

Home Run

The first 'home run' owed a lot to Ant's desire to play a trick on his sister, Sarah. That's the kind of thing you can do if you manage to persuade a TV network to give you an hour on Saturday night to do whatever you like. He probably dreamed this part of the show up as a kid when she was embarrassing him in front of his first girlfriend. While she was playing Bingo with her friends at a large Bingo Hall in Gateshead, Ant and Dec appeared on a giant screen.

'We're very disappointed in you all, going out when we're on the telly,' Ant shook his head.

'Especially you, my sister, Sarah McPartlin! "Oh, I always watch the first show of a series,"' he scoffed as the camera focused on his, only very mildly abashed sibling, "You've got my support Anthony!"'

But Ant and Dec knew that shame alone wouldn't be enough to send the good people of Gateshead rushing back to *Saturday Night Takeaway*. 'I know you people at the Bingo Hall,' Dec said, 'the only way to speak to you is with cold hard cash.'

'The only way to speak to them is just a little bit LOUDER,'

Ant laughed, as some of the more elderly Bingo fans looked somewhat confused.

Still, when they heard about *Saturday Night Takeaway*'s very generous offer, a few of them got up and started edging for the door, and then the edging suddenly turned into a mad rush. At one of their houses were two fat ladies (you see what they've done there?) waiting with £3000 for them in exchange for a simple promise that they'll never leave their house again while Ant and Dec are on TV. It was ingenious. For just £3000 they make dozens of people watch them and all but one won't get any cash at all. Hahaha!

After the success of that first week, though, Ant and Dec got to thinking about all those other ungrateful people who insist on going out on a Saturday night. Don't they realise how much effort goes into *Saturday Night Takeaway*? Don't they know what's it's like to spend your working day with Little Ant and Dec?

From then on they hit a different venue every week: a dog track, a wedding reception, even an aeroplane. Sometimes the one person who'd got money waiting for them didn't even go home, so, for less than the price of one of the Evil Producer's cars they got, probably, hundreds of new viewers. That's more than some stations get for programmes with a budget of, oh, ten times that. . .

The MOULIN

For the first time Ant and Dec actually look pleased when they see this week's 'What's Next?'. The curtain lifts to reveal row upon row of smiling, long-legged dancers doing the cancan. The two presenters can't see any of the usual opportunities for physical or mental torture. And they're looking really, really hard.

'You know, I might like this, this week,' muses Dec.

STARRING MR DECLAN 'FRED ASTAIRE' DONNELLY.

ROUGE

Even better, this week's instructions are in an envelope in one of the dancer's suspender belt. 'I'll get it, I'll get it,' they shout trying to wrestle each other out of the way. Luckily, foreseeing this problem, the producers have provided another envelope and another dancer so they both get a go ('Who needs Little Ant and Dec?' the crew must think to themselves sometimes).

But, as usual, things aren't as straightforward as they seem. Apparently there's a problem. The plan is that they'll join in with a dance but those careless wardrobe people have only managed to come up with one male costume between the two of them – one of them will have to wear a dress. Luckily the producers are nothing if not fair and they've allowed this week's studio audience to vote on who they think it should be.

Ant: 'This was my least favourite after 'Circus Of Horrors'. Only because I drew the short straw and had to dress as one of the girls. I tell you what, **I'm not a fan of those fishnet stockings!** It was pretty embarrassing and as soon as the curtain went up I knew exactly what we'd have to do, but at least the view was good with all the girls. **I'd like to think that the audience voted for me to wear the dress because I'm their favourite, but they probably just wanted to make me look stupid.'**

MOULIN

The whole audience filed into a voting booth on the way into the studio and the result, with 348 votes, was that Ant 'won'. You can see that when they get the news both Ant and Dec are trying to work out what criteria people voted on:

Who they want to see embarrassed?

Who's got the best legs?

Either way, when they come back after the break, Ant looks like a particularly hard-bitten barmaid in a prison production of *Annie Get Your Gun*. Dec, funnily enough, still looks quite happy in his smart suit. When the routine starts, though, he soon realises that the cancan is almost as physically exhausting as the Navy 'What's Next?'.

Most of these girls' legs are longer than his entire body.

IF THIS IS MOULIN ROUGE, WHERE'S KYLIE?

ROUGE

Meanwhile Ant's leg looks like it might break as he tries to raise it above waist height. But, by the end, Dec has got quite cocky and attempts a quick bit of break-dancing to finish off. Ant looks at him with disdain and then jabs a finger at the audience, **'None of you are ever coming to see us again,'** he laughs.

Dec: 'There are so many ways that you can look at the way that vote went. Either everybody likes me and they wanted to make a fool out of Ant, or they thought Ant would look better in a dress, or they all love Ant and didn't quite understand the vote and thought they were voting for their favourite! I try to believe that everybody loves me so they voted for him. That's my theory and I'm sticking to it. I had a really good time because I could see how uncomfortable Ant was in that dress doing the dancing. I'm not sure what he was complaining for because that's how he dresses on a weekend anyway.'

73

Win the Ads 4

Don't Just Watch The Ads, Win Them!

You might have got half the questions right and still only won some toilet roll, a few packets of crisps and one of those stair lifts that they always advertise during *This Morning*. Have another go and see if you can get the car, or at least another Saga holiday...

1 Who presented 2003's *Popstars: The Rivals?*
a Dermot O'Leary
b Davina McCall

2 What was the title of One True Voice's debut single?
a 'Sacred Trust'
b 'A Sacred Love'

3 Which UK Garage sensation's debut single was 'I Luv U'
a Dizzee Rascal
b Lisa Maffia

4 Which actor appeared in both *The Fast Show* and *Cold Feet?*
a James Nesbitt
b John Thomson

5 Who performed the original version of *Brookside* actress Jennifer Ellison's debut single 'Baby I Don't Care'
a Voice Of The Beehive
b Transvision Vamp

6 What was Winona Ryder's excuse after she was caught shoplifting clothes?
a A film director told her to steal them to rehearse for a film
b A mysterious stranger put the items in her bag

7 What was the last band the legendary Phil Spector produced before he was arrested on suspicion of shooting actress Lana Clarkson?
a Coldplay
b Starsailor

8 Who is Arnold Swarzenegger's wife Maria Shriver the niece of?
a Ronald Reagan
b John F Kennedy

9 What did music industry representatives complain was destroying their profits?
a Fans downloading MP3s on the internet
b Increasing recording costs

10 Who sings these lyrics 'You stick in the knife / then give the kiss of life / Live the lie.'
a David Sneddon
b Linkin Park

11 Who sings these lyrics, 'What do I have but negativity / Cause I can't justify the way everyone is looking at me.'
a Linkin Park
b David Sneddon

12 What football team did David Seaman join after leaving Arsenal?
a Bolton Wanderers
b Manchester City

13 In the film *Calender Girls* for what cause were the girls stripping off?
a Cancer Research
b Save The Children

14 Which star attracted a bid of £35,000 from a Ms Joni Rimm for a kiss at an AIDS charity auction?
a George Clooney
b Sharon Stone

15 Which veteran actress made a return to the small screen in *Emmerdale*?
a Lorraine Chase
b Honor Blackman

16 Which pop band was Heidi from the Sugababes originally in?
a Atomic Kitten
b Eternal

17 Which British director was confirmed for the next Harry Potter film?
a Mike Leigh
b Mike Newell

18 What birthday did football manager Bobby Robson celebrate in 2003?
a 60
b 70

19 Who attempted to buy Concorde from British Airways?
a Virgin
b Ryanair

20 20/ Which seventies film reportedly has a sequel in the pipeline?
a *Taxi Driver*
b *Grease*

Undercover Emmerdale

It was an unusually quiet day in Emmerdale. For a change there were no aeroplanes falling on the post office, hard-nosed blondes having catfights, or absurd sideburns to be seen. Luckily, two Jamaican housewives, Patti and Bernice, had won the chance to be extras in the Woolpack for the day and it wasn't going to be quiet for much longer.

To begin with they're quite good. They look a little bit bored but they're just quietly sitting on one side of the Woolpack while Jack, Jerry, Sid, Louise and Diane try to have a serious conversation on the other.

'Hey, let me know if you need another look around.' **Jack is saying gruffly.**

'No, no I've seen enough thanks,' says Sid.

Meanwhile, in the background, Patti and Bernice have decided that they're not getting enough out of this once-in-a-lifetime experience, so they start wandering around the bar, ending up standing directly behind Diane and Louise, who are, coincidentally, just about to come into shot.

'I haven't seen Terry this happy for ages,' says Diane, heroically ignoring the two 'women' behind her.

You call these women's shoes? Purleese!

76

'Oy! Come back, you've missed a bit!'

'Yeah,' replies Louise, 'well I hope he knows what he's doing.'

By now Patti is openly staring at the two actresses, while Bernice has stuck her head around Louise and is gawping at the camera. To the *Emmerdale* cast they probably seem eerily impassive and unimpressed but that might just be because it's hard to look enthusiastic with half an inch of rubber mask stuck to your face.

'Not too keen on wedding plans, I take it?' asks Diane.

'Yeah,' replies Louise, 'well he's big enough to look after himself.'

'I'd've thought you'd be pleased he's moved on.'

'Yeah well, is that why he made a pass at me before he went away?'

It's supposed to be a very serious moment but the two actresses, Emily Symons and Liz Estensen, can't concentrate, they're struggling not to laugh. Luckily, the *Emmerdale* cast are solid professionals, some of these people survived having a plane land on their village, and they're damned if they're going to be put off by two uppity extras. They're sure they can get it right with a second take...

'I haven't seen Terry this happy for ages,' Diane tries again

but behind them Patti and Bernice are now determined to make an impression. They pick up their drinks in a sophisticated, actor-ish manner, but then Bernice spoils things by sticking her tongue out.

'Yeah, well, he's big enough to look after himself.' Louise begins once more but soon they have to put up with an even bigger distraction. Somewhere in the bar a phone starts ringing. It's Patti's.

'**Derek, I can't talk now I'm in the Woolpack,**' she whispers hoarsely, looking understandably embarrassed.

Emily and Liz give up all pretence of following the script, cracking up with laughter.

'**I'm on TV,**' Patti continues, taking no notice. '**I can't talk now I'm on TV. I call you back, Derek.**'

'**Cut!**' snaps the director, resignedly, and they begin '**Take 4**'

'**Hey, let me know if you need another look around,**' Jack starts, right from the beginning.

'**No, no I've seen enough thanks, um,**' Sid stumbles, painfully aware that the crazy Jamaican lady is grinning at him. '**F***! Sorry can we do that again?**'

'**Nobody knows their lines!**' Patti mutters disapprovingly.

At this point she walks around the bar to where the actors are. '**Are we finished?**' she asks plaintively. '**Can we go home now? Thank you for allowing us to be on your TV programme, it was very kind of you.**'

By now the whole cast has realised that something is going on and when Bernice, AKA Ant, falls off his stool they all laugh, thinking that it's part of the act.

'**I'm so sorry,**' s/he laughs as Patti picks her up and drags her away, '**let's get out of here!**'

'**Thank you for letting us be on your TV show,**' Dec / Bernice grins. '**And thank you, all of you, for being on our TV show. *Ant and Dec's Saturday Night Takeaway!***'

Ant: 'Emmerdale was, along with GMTV, the hardest one to do because it was trying to hit people in telly who know what's going on. We were always very conscious of not getting caught. It's like a military operation those things. It's one of those things where you think "That'll be a right laugh!" but the reality is that it's hard work, five hours in a make-up chair, and then wearing it for three or four hours. You're sweaty and you've got a large Jamaican woman's body and women's shoes.'

Dec: 'Yeah, but you got used to that!'

Ant: 'And I really did fall off the stool at the end. They thought that was part of the act as well but it wasn't!'

'Ha ha! Yes, very funny. It took us another 59 takes to get that scene right! Well, from now on, you're barred!'

WHAT'S NEXT?

The Gorillas

A large, empty cage strewn with a little straw. In front of it stands a slim, blonde woman with the kind of soothing smile that friendly dentists use when they're about to remove most of your teeth. She tells an apprehensive Ant and Dec that she works for the 'Los Angeles Primate Sanctuary' looking after two Western Lowland Gorillas called Jessie and Dillan, who, apparently, 'travel the world meeting people and being ambassadors'. If that makes them sound like Mr and Miss World, though, the reality, when the two presenters come back after the break, is very different.

The ape's friend, Dr Gill, warns the audience not to make too much noise. 'So shhhhh!' says Dec pretending that he's joking.

'So please, shut up!!' says Ant, not pretending at all. In the back of the cage there's now a slightly sullen looking gorilla, squatting in a corner and staring at its toes. 'OK guys,' says Dr Gill soothingly, 'we know what we've got to do. Keep talking to them, like I told you, "ooh-ooh-ahh!" Ant and Dec look like they realise that that noise quite possibly means, 'your mother is an orang-utan' in ape-speak, but they begin nervously edging towards the big ape, holding out the sticks of celery they've been given as presents / extremely ineffective weapons.

your mother is an

Luckily for Dec Jessie seems to have taken a fancy to him and she begins playfully throwing straw over his head. **'She's playing with you there!'** says Dr Gill, helpfully. **'Naughty girl Jessie! Good girl Jessie!'** Jessie then hands Dec a banana. 'If you take that you have to eat it, you really need to eat it,' she warns him, her voice rising as it doesn't look like he's going to eat the banana in time. Dec practically swallows the banana whole.

If they thought Jessie was a little over-friendly, though, just wait until they meet Dillan, who enters the cage next. **'This is our Silverback, he's about 300 – 350 pounds,'** says Dr Gill. Dillan seems very keen on Ant. 'OK, he's sniffing your butt, but that's fine, no problem at all,' she continues. That's a matter of opinion, thinks Ant, as Dillan pushes him headfirst down into the straw and then practically insists that he scratch his back. **'That's the two of you, live on TV, grooming gorillas,'** says Dr Gill happily.

Anyone for celery?

'Right, OK, I think it's time to get you out of there now,' decides Dr Gill as the two apes show signs of being bored with their massage. Ant and Dec edge slowly towards the door and then sprint desperately through it. 'OK guys well done,' she tells them, warmly. 'But our gorillas have got something to show you!'

From somewhere 'I Wanna Be Like You' from *The Jungle Book* starts up and Jessie and Dillan begin dancing, arm in arm. At last Ant and Dec realise that they've been set up. Or at least they should do. 'How did she teach them to do the dance at the end, Dec?' laughs Ant, 'that's what I don't understand!'

WHAT'S NEXT?

Ant: 'That was the most scared I've ever been! When we were getting changed, I could hear the warm-up guy telling the audience:"Be deadly silent, we don't want you clapping, we don't want you cheering because it could be potentially dangerous for Ant and Dec". Then the executive producer's pacing up and down going: "Oh, is this a good idea? I don't know if this is a good idea!" while we're getting changed into these gloves and boiler-suits so that we're not going to get harmed by the gorillas. There are even two bouncers there so that if the gorillas go too mad they can drag them off us – like they're going to be any help! Everything led us to believe that it was real.'

Dec: 'They felt really strong and muscular and their hands were veiny, and the smell, everything was so realistic. When they gave me the banana and she said: "You have to eat it!" I was like: "I'll eat it! I'll shove it up my a***
if you like!"'

Ant: 'And there was us two holding out our sticks of celery like they'd protect us from a Silver Back Gorilla. "Get back! Get back! On guard!" And that stupid noise! People still do that to us in the pub, now. You try and win an argument and you think: "I've got you there!" and they go, "Ooh-ah! ooh-ah!" There's no riposte to that.'

Ant & Dec... Kings of the swingers

have a banana

Make-overs
Ron and Yvonne

It's amazing how much care and attention can go into making someone look so ugly. Of course the really great Saturday Night Entertainers, your Jeremy Beadles and Noel Edmonds, never needed a makeover.

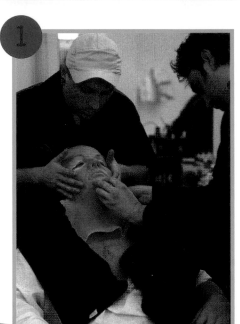

Has Ant just been Tango-ed?

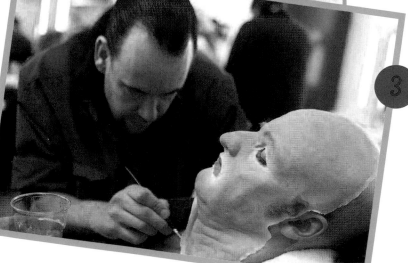

Even Dr Frankenstein might have some doubts about this monster. It's alive, but only just.

Get the LOOK!

Yes, Yvonne's wig is on the right way round.

5

4

Teams of make-up artists worked for hours on Yvonne but sadly she still looks a little bit like the Cowardly Lion from *The Wizard Of Oz*.

6

The Finished Look

Saucy Yvonne knows how to turn the paparazzi to jelly.

Pop stars

Jim never fixed it for Ant to perform with Madness but luckily the producers found his letter and made his dream come true. Here you can see Suggs saying, 'no, we're not going to sing "Let's Get Ready To Rhumble" now, get back to the back of the stage'

Gareth Gates owes a lot to Ant and Dec who've supported his career ever since Pop Idol. That's why he didn't mind when they made him dress up as a fur-coat wearing prima donna the first time they invited him on the show, or that Dec tried to steal his dinner money the second time. Or at least they hope he didn't mind …

When Westlife came in to perform on *Saturday Night Takeaway* they didn't expect to find themselves chained to a table, watching an entire week's worth of Ads. Good of Ant and Dec to look so concerned as a TV explodes in their face.

Shania Twain was just one of the pop legends who was lured on the show with the promise of meeting Little Ant and Dec. That week Little Ant and Dec had to be lured on to the show with the promise that they wouldn't meet Shania.

1

The smell in the 'gorillas' cage came from Elephant dung imported from London Zoo.

2

While queuing up for his audition for *American Idol* Dec was dragged away to be interviewed by an unsuspecting Paula Abdul .

6

The body suits that Ant and Dec wear to become Patti and Bernice weigh 115 pounds.

5

Kenny and George's wigs alone cost £1000 to make

3

Originally Little Ant was chosen to be Little Dec. The two of them are school friends in real life.

4

After filming, Ant and Dec used to like to remain in character as Kenny and George, finding it hilarious to swear at each other in cockney.

Saturday Night Takeaway'

8

The producers saw over 300 potential Little Ant and Decs before settling on the final two.

7

At one point the production team considered doing a 'what's next?' that involved Ant having his chest waxed and Dec having his legs waxed. Fortunately they decided not to do it on the grounds of taste and decency.

9

Little Ant and Dec were invited to the Oscars, but couldn't go because of school commitments.

10

If you look carefully during the performance of Gustav and Jurgen on *This Morning*, you can see that Ant's lip falls off.

Win the Ads the answers

So how many ads would you have won?

Quiz 1

pages 24-25

Answers

1/ b	2/ a	3/ a	4/ a	5/b
6/b	7/a	8/a	9/b	10/b
11/a	12/a	13/b	14/a	15/b
16/a	17/b	18/b	19/b	20/b

Quiz 2

pages 48–49

Answers

1/ b	2/ a	3/ a	4/ a	5/ b
6/ b	7/ a	8/ b	9/ a	10/a
11/ a	12/ a	13/ b	14/ b	15/ b
16/ a	17/ a	18/ a	19/ b	20/ a

Quiz 3

pages 66–67

Answers

1/ a	2/ a	3/ b	4/ a	5/ b
6/ a	7/ b	8/ a	9/ b	10/ a
11/ a	12/ a	13/ b	14/ b	15/ a
16/ a	17/ b	18/ a	19/ a	20/ a

Quiz 4

pages 74–75

Answers

1/b	2/a	3/a	4/b	5/b
6/a	7/b	8/a	9/a	10/a
11/a	12/b	13/a	14/b	15/a
16/a	17/b	18/b	19/a	20/b

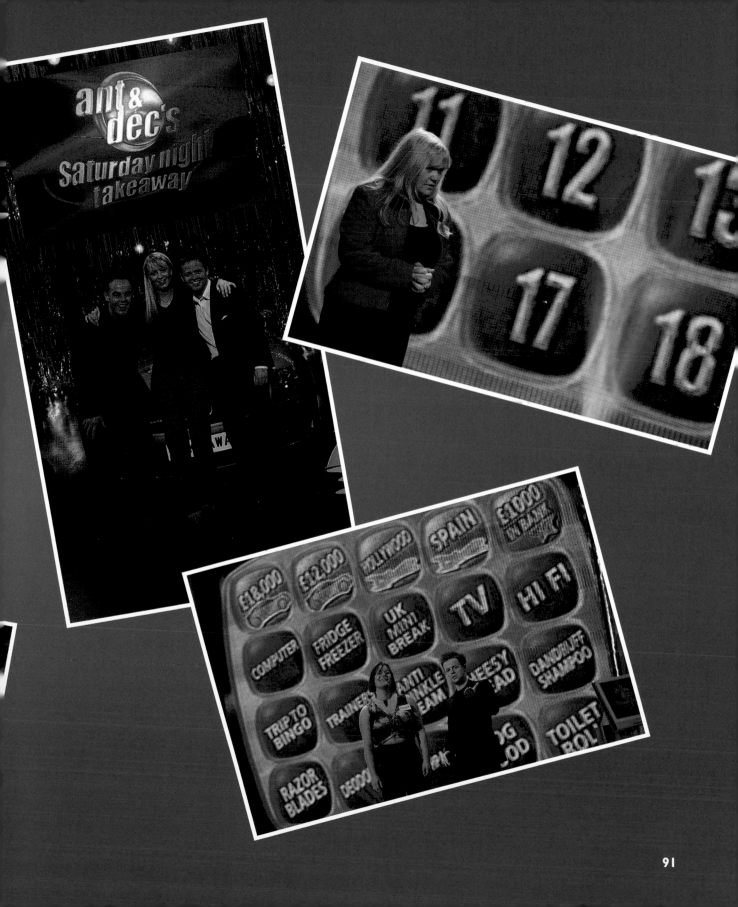

'Don't Just Watch The Ads .. Win A VIP trip to 2004's Saturday Night Takeaway

The only people who have almost as much fun as Ant and Dec on *Saturday Night Takeaway* are the studio audience. Not only do they get to see all the same stuff you see on TV they also see the floor manager getting twitchy as Ant 'pretends' to forget his lines, or the cameramen sniggering uncontrollably as Dec is menaced by a man in a gorilla suit. Well, get the 20 questions here right and you could win four 'VIP' tickets to any show in the next series, and future bragging rights till you're at least 105...

To enter the prize draw, put your name, address & answers on a postcard to:

Ant and Dec's Saturday Night Takeaway
Competition
Marketing Department, Carlton Books Ltd,
20 Mortimer Street, London W1T 3JW

Closing Date: 31/12/03

The winner will be the first
correct answer drawn
on the 6/1/04

The Questions

 1 **Who played The Terminatrix in**
Terminator III?
a   Joanna Hoken
b   Kristanna Loken

 2 **Which singer did Catalina impersonate in**
the Stars In Their Eyes I'm A Celebrity ...
Get Me Out Of Here! Special?
a   Madonna
b   Debbie Harry

 3 **Which sitcom did Ant and Dec**
once remake an episode from?
a   The Likely Lads
b   On The Buses

4 **Who did Coldplay singer Chris Martin**
reportedly propose to this year?
a   Gwyneth Paltrow
b   Jennifer Aniston

5 **On what show did Hayley Evetts**
first catch the public eye?
a   Pop Idol
b   Neighbours

 6 **What was Nikki Chapman's day job**
before she became a judge on
Pop Idol?
a   Publicist
b   Nightclub owner

 7 **What was the name of the model**
that Jordan had a tabloid row with?
a   Susie Pond
b   Jodie Marsh

8 **Who duetted with Blu Cantrell on the**
chart-topper 'Breathe'
a   Nelly
b   Sean Paul

9 **According to Busted in 'The Year**
3000' who is pretty fine?
a   "your great great great great
granddaughter"
b   "your great great great granddaughter"

10 **On what show did Delta Goodrem**
make her name?
a   Neighbours
b   Pop Idol

11 **What did Michael Douglas and**
Catherine Zeta Jones call their
daughter?
a   Cerys
b   Bronwynn

12 **Which EastEnders actor turned up on**
the beat in The Bill?
a   Todd Carty
b   Ross Kemp

13 **Which punk band had a hit with 'The Tide Is High' before Atomic Kitten?**
a *Blondie*
b *Siouxsie and the Banshees*

 14 **How much money was Chris Evans forced to pay Virgin Radio?**
a £7 million
b £10 million

15 **Which horror stars battled it out on the big screen this year?**
a Freddie vs Jason
b Dracula vs Wolfman

16 **What did film star Angelina Jolie throw away after breaking up with husband Billy Bob Thornton?**
a the preserved head of his great-grandfather that he gave her as a wedding gift
b the vial of his blood that she used to wear around her neck

17 **Who directed *Kill Bill*?**
a Robert Rodriguez
b Quentin Tarantino

 18 **According to Electric Six's hit 'Danger! High Voltage' there's "fire in the disco / fire in the gates of hell" and where else?**
a "the Taco-Bell"
b "the sleepy knell"

 19 **Which book knocked the fifth Harry Potter off the best-seller spot?**
a Stephen Schama's *A History Of Britain*
b Dr Robert Atkins' *Diet Revolution*

20 **What did Ant say was his least favourite 'What's Next?' during last year's *Saturday Night Takeaway*?**
a The Gorillas
b The Circus Of Horrors